LOOKING BEYOND

Steve Parker

Published by Smart Apple Media, an imprint of Black Rabbit Books
P.O. Box 3263, Mankato, Minnesota 56002
www.blackrabbitbooks.com

Produced by David West ☂ Children's Books
6 Princeton Court, 55 Felsham Road, London SW15 1AZ

Designed by Gary Jeffrey

Cataloging-in-Publication Data is available from the Library of Congress.
ISBN 978-1-62588-076-5

CSPIA compliance information: DWCB14FCP
011014

9 8 7 6 5 4 3 2 1

All images courtesy of NASA except: p1, NASA, ESA, and the Hubble SM4 ERO Team; p6tl, NASA / WMAP Science Team, p6b, ESA and the Planck Collaboration; p7t, ESO/M. Kornmesser, p7b, NASA, ESA, S. Beckwith (STScI) and the HUDF Team, p7b (inset), Space Telescope Science Institute and the European Space Agency; p8r, NASA, ESA, M. Livio and the Hubble 20th Anniversary Team (STScI), p8mr, Nathan Smith (University of California, Berkeley), and NASA; p9tl, ESA/Hubble & NASA Acknowledgement Jean-Christophe Lambry, p9r, NASA, ESA and AURA/Caltech, p9ml, Casey Reed/NASA, p9mr, p9b, p13b, p19t, p21tr, NASA/JPL-Caltech; p10tl, (STScI/AURA) and R. Sahai and J. Trauger (Jet Propulsion Laboratory), p10t, p13tl, p15tl, p15tr, NASA and the Hubble Heritage Team (AURA/STScI), p10mr, NASA, ESA, Andrew Fruchter (STScI), and the ERO team (STScI + ST-ECF, p10bl, ESA/NASA; p11t, ESA/Hubble & NASA, p11r, NASA, ESA, J. Hester and A. Loll (Arizona State University), p11m, NASA/ESA and G. Bacon (STScI), p11b, NASA, ESA, D. Lennon and E. Sabbi (ESA/STScI), J. Anderson, S. E. de Mink, R. van der Marel, T. Sohn, and N. Walborn (STScI), N. Bastian (Excellence Cluster, Munich), L. Bedin (INAF, Padua), E. Bressert (ESO), P. Crowther (University of Sheffield), A. de Koter (University of Amsterdam), C. Evans (UKATC/STFC, Edinburgh), A. Herrero (IAC, Tenerife), N. Langer (AifA, Bonn), I. Platais (JHU), and H. Sana (University of Amsterdam); p12tl, UNAM), R. Smith (NOAO/CTIO), S. Snowden (NASA/GSFC) and G. Ramos-Larios (IAM), p12bl, April Hobart, CXC, p12br, p18m, p23m, ESO/L. Calçada; p13m, L. Ferrarese (Johns Hopkins University) and NASA, p13r, X-ray (NASA/CXC/MIT/C.Canizares, M.Nowak); Optical (NASA/STScI); p14, p15mr, p15bl, p15b, p18tl, NASA, ESA, and The Hubble Heritage Team (STScI/AURA), p14tr, ESA/Hubble & NASA, p14m, Project Investigators for the original Hubble data: K.D. Kuntz (GSFC), F. Bresolin (University of Hawaii), J. Trauger (JPL), J. Mould (NOAO), and Y.-H. Chu (University of Illinois, Urbana) Image processing: Davide De Martin (ESA/Hubble) CFHT image: Canada-France-Hawaii Telescope/J.-C. Cuillandre/Coelum NOAO image: George Jacoby, Bruce Bohannan, Mark Hanna/NOAO/AURA/NSF, p14l, J. Blakeslee (Washington State University); p15ml, p16br, p18b, ESO, p15br, ALMA (ESO-NAOJ-NRAO)-NASA-ESA Hubble Space Telescope; p16t, ESO-Y. Beletsky, p16tr, X-ray: NASA/UMass/Q.D.Wang et al.; Optical: NASA/STScI/AURA/Hubble Heritage; Infrared: NASA/JPL-Caltech/Univ. AZ/R.Kennicutt/SINGS Team, p16m, NASA/JPL-Caltech/ESO/R. Hurt; p17t, ESO-S. Guisard, p17ml, NRAO/AUI, p17mr, Adam Evans, p17b, Hewholooks; p18m (inset), C.R. O'Dell/Rice University; NASA, p18m, D. Aguilar-Harvard-Smithsonian Center for Astrophysics; p19m, b, NASA/JPL-Caltech/T. Pyle (SSC/Caltech); p20tl, p21tl, Ron Miller/NASAblueshift, p20tr, NASA/Ames/JPL-Caltech, p20m, NASA, ESA, M. Kornmesser, p20l, ESA - C.Carreau, p20b, NASA/ESA/G. Bacon; p21t, Haven Giguere-Yale, p21l, NASA/ESA and G. Bacon (STScI); p22l, Carter Roberts, p22r, NASA and Ball Aerospace; p24t, NASA/MSFC, p24l, NASA/Advanced Concepts Lab; p25m, Space X, p25b, NASA Glenn Research Center; p26b (& inset), ESA-Foster + Partners; p27 main, Mars One/Bryan Versteeg

CONTENTS

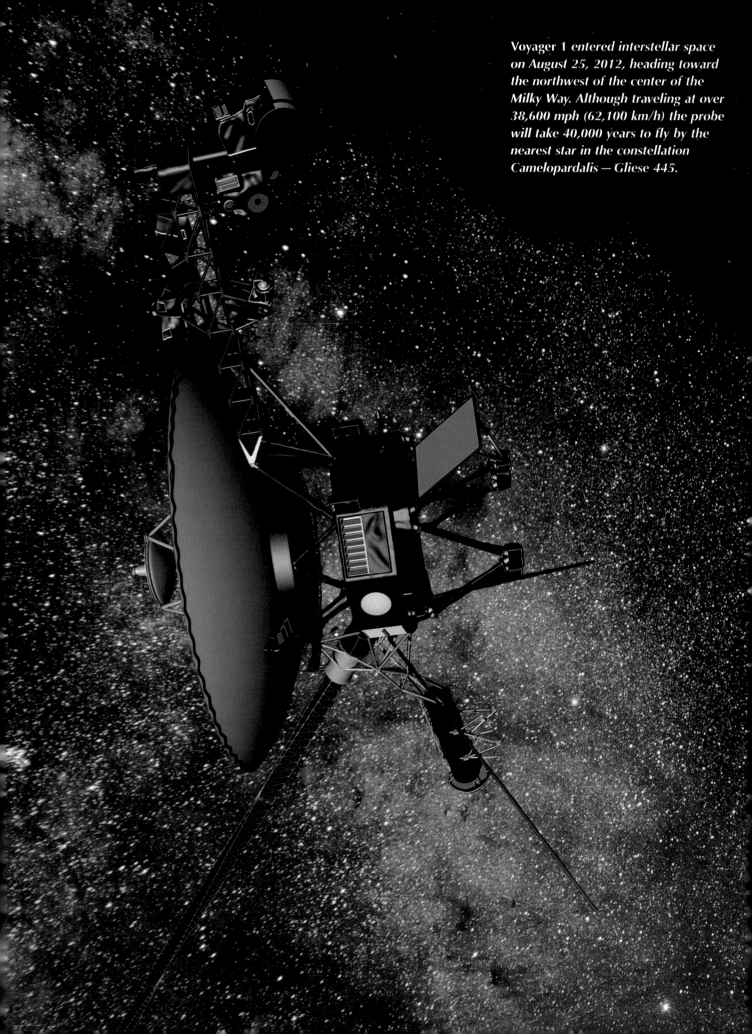

Voyager 1 entered interstellar space on August 25, 2012, heading toward the northwest of the center of the Milky Way. Although traveling at over 38,600 mph (62,100 km/h) the probe will take 40,000 years to fly by the nearest star in the constellation Camelopardalis — Gliese 445.

INTRODUCTION

Beyond our Solar System lie 300 billion stars in our home galaxy, the Milky Way. Yet the Milky Way is only one among hundreds of billions of galaxies in the known Universe. The nearest star to our Sun is over 24 trillion miles (38 trillion kilometers) away, and reaching it is far beyond our current technology. But the 21st century is bringing amazing advances in our exploration of deep space. We have found alien planets, studied black holes, and gained insights into the origins of the Universe itself. What incredible events will the coming years bring?

Planets beyond our Solar System range from rare gas giants several times larger than Jupiter, to more common Neptune-sized planets, to less numerous smaller planets or "Super-Earths." These last kinds, like those orbiting in the triple star system of Gliese 667, are the best candidates for supporting life.

NASA *Wilkinson Microwave Anisotropy Probe (WMAP)*

Reflectors

Optics

Solar array

THE BIG BANG

In the 1920s US astronomer Edwin Hubble discovered that the Universe is expanding—very fast. This meant, back in time, galaxies were much closer together. In fact, go back far enough and all matter and energy must have been in one tiny place.

Launched in 2001, WMAP measured traces of microwave background radiation left from the Big Bang. The cooler blue areas are where gravity first caused matter to collapse and form stars.

EPIC EXPANSION

Imagine the future entire Universe within one original particle, smaller than a single atom. Then 13.8 billion years ago it erupted in the Big Bang. In a tiny fraction of a second it became the size of a grapefruit with two of the Universe's basic forces, gravity and the strong nuclear force. A microsecond later this expanded as a fizzing cauldron of energy and particles, trillions of degrees hot, with the two other basic forces, weak nuclear and electromagnetic.

A visual timeline of the Universe from its origin, 13.8 billion years ago.

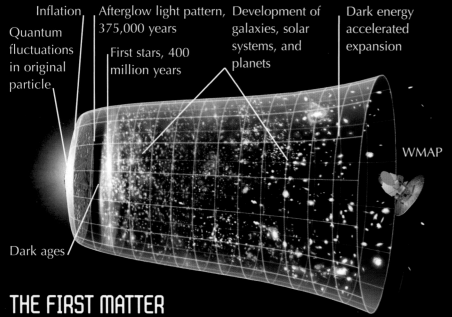

Inflation

Quantum fluctuations in original particle

Afterglow light pattern, 375,000 years

First stars, 400 million years

Development of galaxies, solar systems, and planets

Dark energy accelerated expansion

WMAP

Dark ages

THE FIRST MATTER

Still, after less than one second, the Universe cooled enough for fundamental particles called quarks to combine. They formed atomic particles such as protons and electrons as a vast, dark fog of hydrogen. After three minutes it was cool enough for protons to link with neutrons and electrons, forming atoms of helium gas. By 400,000 years the Universe, now "cool" at 4,900 °F (2,700 °C), glowed with the first light.

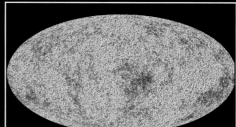

*The European Space Agency's **Planck** spacecraft recently produced an even more detailed "heat map" of the Universe. The denser areas probably came from tiny fluctuations within the original particle, before it inflated after the Big Bang.*

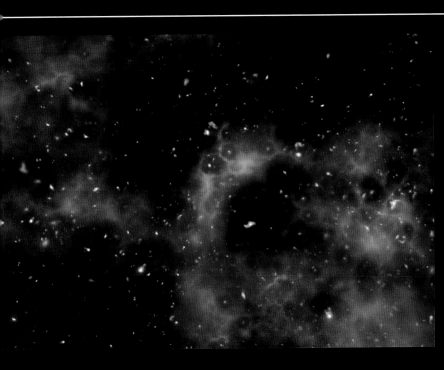

At one billion years old, the early Universe resembled a gigantic nebula (space cloud) dotted with newly forming galaxies lit from within by the massed ignition of trillions of stars.

COSMIC STUFF

As confirmed by the *WMAP* and *Planck* probes, ordinary matter—atoms and molecules—accounts for less than 5% of the Universe. The rest is made up of 27% dark matter and 68% dark energy. As the Universe expands, ordinary matter, energy, and dark matter lose density while dark energy (which is evenly distributed everywhere) stays the same. Over the last six billion years the Universe has been flying apart at an increasing speed as dark energy becomes more and more dominant.

The **UNIVERSE** is **expanding FASTER** than ever—**propelled** by mysterious **DARK ENERGY**.

PEERING INTO THE PAST

Studying starlight shows that chemical elements like helium leave markers in the light spectrum, from red to violet. The longer starlight takes to travel to us, the more these markers shift into the spectrum's red end, known as Red Shift. The most distant stars we can see, with the Hubble Space Telescope, are estimated to be 12 billion light years away. So we see them as they were just after the Universe began. The farthest galaxies are also moving away the fastest. Probably, in 11 billion years the Universe will have vanished!

This is just one small section of the Hubble Ultra Deep Field View. The light from galaxies took so long to get here, we see them as they existed a just few hundred thousand years after the Big Bang.

STAR BIRTH

Stars are the building blocks of galaxies, and even life, across the Universe—cosmic nuclear reactors that light up the heavens.

IGNITION

Stars are born deep within hydrogen-rich dust clouds, when violent movements create a knotty mass that falls inward under its own gravity. The center heats, flaring into a protostar—more commonly, two or three protostars. Gas surrounding the protostar collapses toward it, forming a blazing-hot core. Here massive gravity and pressure force hydrogen atoms together to fuse into helium atoms.

Stars are grouped according to their brightness and color, forming a scale called the Main Sequence. The richness of the surrounding cloud determines how rapidly the star grows and how hot it burns. But greatness comes at a price—the bigger the star, the more quickly it exhausts its fuel. Hypergiant stars can flare and die in a few million years. Our own medium-sized Sun should last 10 billion years.

Vast dusty clouds of gas show new stars breaking free at their tips in the highly active Carina Nebula.

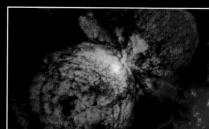

Stars are graded by heat color from O-blue to B, A, F, G, K, L, M, and T-red. Huge Eta Carinae (Type O, above), surrounded by gas, had a "phantom supernova" in the 1840s.

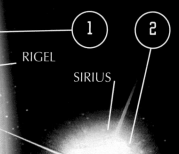

On the size spectrum, Sirius, brightest in our night sky, has twice the mass of our Sun, yet is tiny next to giant Rigel. Barnard's Star is slightly larger than planet Jupiter.

RIGEL

SIRIUS

THE SUN EPSILON ERIDANI BARNARD'S STAR

MAIN SEQUENCE STARS

1. **TYPE B BLUE SUPERGIANT**
2. **TYPE A WHITE STAR**
3. **TYPE G YELLOW DWARF**
4. **TYPE K ORANGE DWARF**
5. **TYPE M RED DWARF**

> ## *"High-luminosity stars are outnumbered by low-luminosity stars a thousand to one."*
> Neil deGrasse Tyson, astrophysicist

Some stars are so hot and massive they begin to smolder. Campbell's Hydrogen Star (HD 184738) has surface temperatures up to 40 times higher than our Sun but it is rapidly shedding its matter. The main light it gives off is ultraviolet.

STAR BEHAVIOR

Star clusters are formed in dense molecular clouds when massive stars are drawn together under their own gravitational attraction. Occasionally one of their number reaches escape velocity to become a runaway.

Cepheid and RR Lyrae stars are evolving stars that pulsate by actually expanding and contracting in size as their energy output varies. Pulsating stars have helped astronomers measure the Universe.

The Pleiades cluster of 1,000-plus stars will remain together for 250 million years. Then the Milky Way's gravity will force them apart.

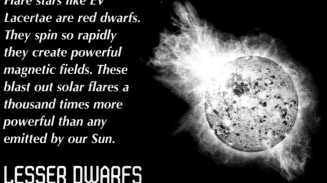

Flare stars like EV Lacertae are red dwarfs. They spin so rapidly they create powerful magnetic fields. These blast out solar flares a thousand times more powerful than any emitted by our Sun.

LESSER DWARFS

Giant runaway star Zeta Ophiuchi plows through space, forcing a bow wave of gas ahead of it. Zeta Ophiuchi is thought to be from a binary system whose partner exploded, propelling the survivor to wander interstellar space.

Stars with half the mass of our Sun or less will burn as either red or brown dwarfs. Red dwarfs make up 75% of the stars in our galaxy but none can be seen by the naked eye—the largest known shine only one-tenth as brightly as our Sun. These low-heat, slow-burning stars will last for trillions of years before their fuel is exhausted.

Brown dwarfs are approximately the same size as Jupiter but are tens of times more massive.

Brown dwarfs are even smaller "failed stars." They fuse heavier fuels, deuterium or lithium, in their cores. Despite their name, they emit light ranging from orange to red.

> The **UNIVERSE** is **YOUNG enough** that **no RED DWARF stars** have **yet PERISHED.**

STAR DEATH

In five billion years, our Sun's core will collapse and heat escaping hydrogen to create runaway fusion. The Sun will expand into a stellar colossus—a red giant.

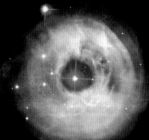

Aging binary star V838 Mon expels a cloud of dusty gas as it enters its death throes. This engulfs its binary partner and their planets.

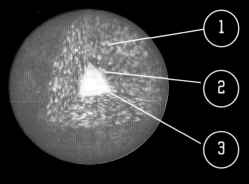

ELEMENTAL FURNACE

In the future Sun's collapsing core, temperatures will rise to 1.8 million F (1 million C). Helium atoms then fuse, jumping the temperature to 180 million F (100 million C) and creating the life-based element carbon. In the furnace of the core, helium nuclei fuse with carbon nuclei to create atoms of oxygen.

After another million years, when helium fusion ceases, the Sun's shell will blow outward in a colorful "planetary" nebula. More massive stars would continue the fusion process beyond oxygen, forging all the elements up to iron. A dense iron core then forms over two days, until collapsing in seconds to explode 26 elements into space. The remnants of the core will be a white dwarf star made of carbon/oxygen or helium—and take billions of years to cool.

INSIDE A TYPICAL RED GIANT

1. **CONVECTIVE ZONE** Heat spreads in circular currents of plasma as the star's envelope swells
2. **BURNING SHELL** Hydrogen burns in a layer around the core, inflating the envelope
3. **CORE** In a star like the Sun, the core cools, helium fusion stops, and the core becomes inert

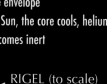

RIGEL (to scale)

If the nearby supermassive red giant Betelgeuse was placed in our Solar System, the outside of its enlarged gaseous shell would reach almost to the orbit of Jupiter.

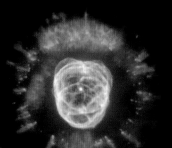

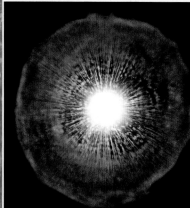

U Cam, a rare carbon star, is shown encased in a bubble of expelled gas as helium begins fusing at its core. The actual size of the red giant would be seen as a tiny dot in the center, but its radiance overwhelmed the Hubble Space Telescope's sensor.

A tiny hot white dwarf sits in the center of a planetary nebula. Despite being from a star, a "planetary" nebula is so-called because astronomers once thought these patterns of ionized gas were made by newly forming planets.

BETELGEUSE

The immediate (15-year) aftermath of a supernova in a nearby dwarf galaxy shows a shockwave of energy igniting a cloud of ejected gas around the exploded star. Such a rare event is yet to be witnessed in detail in our galaxy.

"Every atom in your body came from a star. We are all stardust." Professor Lawrence M. Krauss

Hidden deep in the middle of the supernova remnant called the Crab Nebula is a pulsar. This is a neutron star that emits strong radio signals as it spins 1,000 times each minute.

GOING SUPERNOVA

Only stars with masses between 0.3 times smaller and eight times larger than our Sun will become typical red giants. When the iron core of an even greater monster like Betelgeuse falls in on itself, at 20 million miles (32 million km) per hour, it gets so hot and dense that all its protons and electrons fuse into neutrons.

The ball of neutrons—the hardest, densest substance in the Universe—then almost instantly rebounds with a gargantuan shockwave. The outer layers of the star, at billions of degrees, creates in a fiery instant all the elements heavier than iron. The whole star explodes—a supernova.

It is **estimated** that **TWO** neutron stars **COLLIDING** can **make THREE MOON'S worth** of **GOLD.**

NEUTRON STAR

Only a small number of stars are massive enough to "go supernova." All that is usually left is a fast-spinning object so dense, it contains a mass as heavy as our Sun in a sphere the size of a small city—a neutron star. Colliding neutron stars make heavy, rare elements such as gold and platinum.

A host of new stars ignite into life in the element-rich debris of the Tarantula Nebula as the endless cycle of stellar death and rebirth continues.

BLACK HOLES

Very rarely, a supernova creates a neutron star so massive that it generates a gravitational field impossible to resist. The neutrons in the star are forced so close together they become a singularity.

Massive dying stars called Wolf Rayet stars, like HD50896, are candidates for leaving behind not a tiny neutron star, but a black hole.

At the moment of collapse into a singularity, a neutron star jets out two powerful gamma rays from its poles at 99% the speed of light. An event like this nearby in our galaxy would wipe all life from Earth.

WHERE TIME STOPS

The study of singularities is where our current scientific models of cosmic physics run into problems. Gravitational singularities are so crushingly dense they appear to bend the fabric of the Universe itself to the point where the fastest particles—photons of light—become trapped inside a black hole. At the edge, or event horizon, of a black hole you would actually see not a hole, but a fixed image of the neutron star just before it crushed itself out of normal existence. Nearby objects not traveling fast enough would be irresistibly pulled in and "spaghettified" (stretched infinitely long and thin) by gravity.

NASA's NuStar probe, launched in 2012, is the first dedicated high-energy X-ray telescope. It hunts for black holes in our galaxy.

STELLAR MASS BLACK HOLE

1. **HOST STAR** Orbiting close to the black hole
2. **ACCRETION DISC** Made of star matter
3. **SINGULARITY** Ringed by event horizon
4. **PARTICLE JET** Ultra high-energy photons from compressed solar material

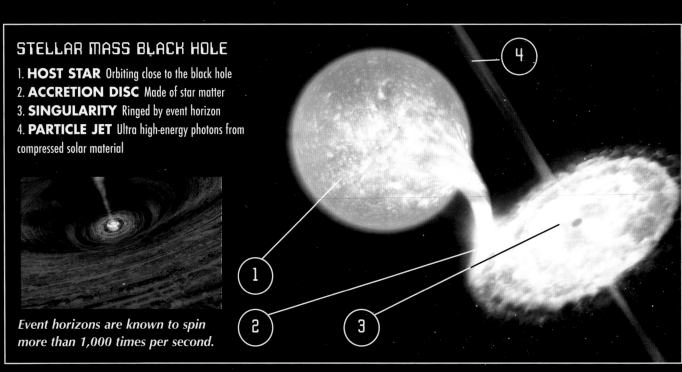

Event horizons are known to spin more than 1,000 times per second.

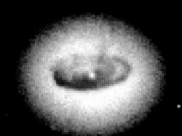

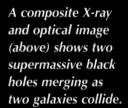

This slightly fuzzy Hubble image (left) shows a ring of gas and dust circling a suspected supermassive black hole at the center of NGC 4261.

In another Hubble image (left), high-energy particles stream from a supermassive black hole six billion times heavier than our Sun. It is at the center of nearby galaxy Messier 87.

A composite X-ray and optical image (above) shows two supermassive black holes merging as two galaxies collide.

SUPERMASSIVES

Stellar-mass black holes are made by a single star up to 33 times more massive than our Sun. Our home galaxy, the Milky Way, contains at least 100 million stellar-mass black holes, but so far only about 12 are known to us. Supermassive black holes can be hundreds of thousands to billions of times more massive. Exactly how they form is a mystery. But they are thought to lurk at the center of most galaxies, attracting vast swathes of stars and nebulae to rotate around them.

A **QUASAR** is about the **size** of our **SOLAR SYSTEM** but **emits** more **ENERGY** than the **entire MILKY WAY.**

The part of the Universe we can see contains 100 billion galaxies. Some of the brightest and farthest harbor supermassive black holes that power quasars. These distant, active galactic centers emit the most powerful particle streams in the Universe.

Supermassive black holes are thought to kill off star formation in elliptical galaxies by blasting away gas-rich nebulae. An increase in supermassives may play a key role in the eventual fate of the Universe.

GALAXIES

A galaxy is a gathering of stars, star remnants, dust, and nebulae that circulate around a massive center. Galaxies come in all sizes, shapes, and ages.

HOW GALAXIES GROW

Galaxies grow from clumps of dark matter that gravitationally attract gas and dust. Dark matter, by its nature, cannot expand and contract. So as the massing gas cloud falls inward, it forces the dark matter out to its edges, allowing the cloud to gain mass and spin itself into a wide, thin, spiraling disc. The most massive spiral galaxies absorb smaller galaxies as they travel, eventually gaining so many stars they turn into formless blobs called elliptical galaxies. The odd-shaped irregular galaxies are thought to be formed from chance galactic collisions.

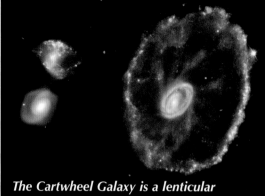

The Cartwheel Galaxy is a lenticular galaxy—an in-between shape formed as a spiral slowly changes into an elliptical. It was then punched through the middle by a smaller galaxy causing a visible shockwave.

SPIRAL GALAXY M101

1. **SPIRAL ARM** Full of hot blue stars forming
2. **DUST LANES** Drawn into spiral pattern by gravity
3. **CENTRAL BULGE** Concentration of older, low-mass stars, equivalent to 3 billion masses of our Sun
4. **INTERSTELLAR MEDIUM** Gas, dust, cosmic rays

The Pinwheel Galaxy is a typical spiral. Located 21 million light-years away in Ursa Minor, its spirals are very active. Unusually, it may not have a black hole at its center.

In elliptical galaxies, star-making gases have become thin and diffuse. The old, low-mass stars here no longer rotate around a central core. The massive elliptical galaxy ESO 325-G004 contains 100 billion stars but very little new star formation.

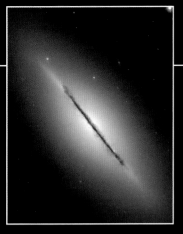

The Spindle Galaxy is a lenticular galaxy viewed from the side. A long, thick cloud of dust cuts through a hazy center full of thinned gases and aging stars.

In Galaxy M64 the dark bands of gas that rotate in the opposite direction to its stars probably came from a galaxy absorbed long ago.

CLUSTERS

Galaxies are not evenly distributed across the Universe. They are clumped together in superclusters, attracted by epic filaments of dark matter that run through the Universe like great webs. The most numerous types of galaxies seen in our Virgo supercluster are spiral or irregular, which are typical for this low-density area of the Universe.

NGC2207

To be **classed** as a **GALAXY**, a **STAR CLUSTER** needs to have at least **10 MILLION stars**.

IC2163

These two spiral galaxies (left) in our supercluster are about to merge. Larger NGC2207 has started stripping stars from smaller IC2163. In one billion years they will be one huge elliptical.

The Antennae Galaxies NGC 4038 and 4039 (below) are also merging spirals. Although actual stars do not collide, their gas and dust clouds do, creating mass ignition of new stars shrouded in pink ionized hydrogen. A combined wavelength image (inset) shows an abundance of the elements neon, magnesium, and silicon.

Star-birthing regions

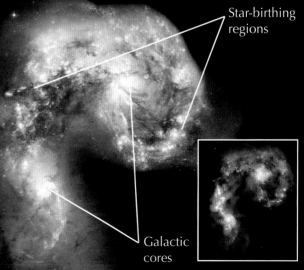

A small section of spiral galaxy NGC 300 shows stars as numerous as grains of sand on a beach.

Galactic cores

OUR GALAXY

Our home galaxy, the Milky Way, was named by ancient Greeks. They thought this dense strip of stars resembled a celestial river of milk.

AN AVERAGE BARRED SPIRAL

The Milky Way is a spiral galaxy about 120,000 light-years in diameter. In the center is a well defined "bulge"—a dense mass of old and new stars. From here extends a bar of stars and gas into two main spiral arms, the Sagittarius Arm

A spiral galaxy viewed side on shows its central bulge, dust-less halo, and surrounding globular clusters.

and the Centaurus Arm. Other, lesser spirals of gas, dust, and star-making activity also radiate from the center.

Our Solar System sits in the quiet Orion Spur of the Perseus Arm, 27,000 light-years from the center. Above and below the galaxy's main disc, globular clusters orbit—compact masses of old stars. Parts of the Milky Way are 13.2 billion years old—nearly as aged as the Universe itself.

A telescope in Chile aims a laser directly toward the center of the Milky Way. The southern hemisphere offers the best Earth-based views of our galaxy.

Solar System

PERSEUS

ORION

OUTER ARM

ORION SPUR

CARINA-SAGITTARIUS

SCUTUM-CENTAURUS

GALACTIC BAR

Kepler search space (see page 22)

Omega Centauri is by far the largest globular cluster in the Milky Way. It is thought to be the leftover core of a dwarf galaxy that was absorbed eons ago.

> *"...nothing seems special about our Galaxy, our Local Group—such is our niche in the Universe."*
> Eric J. Chaisson, astrophysicist and science educator

A vast dust lane obscures our optical view of the Milky Way's center. The exact makeup of galactic dust is unknown but it is thought to come from dead and dying stars.

COSMIC WHIRLPOOL

Our Solar System, along with the rest of the Milky Way, rotates around the supermassive black hole hidden in its Galactic Center. Rotation speed is 600,000 miles (970,000 km) per hour, meaning the Solar System completes one orbit every 200 million years. So we have gone one-third of the way around since the extinction of the dinosaurs. From oddities in rotation, we know our galaxy is made up of 90% dark matter.

Sagittarius A* is a bright point of intense radiation hidden behind layers of dust in the Galactic Center (left). Radio telescopes reveal spiraling flares of ionized gas while the object itself remains motionless. Infrared images show stars orbiting the object at colossal speed. Only a supermassive black hole could cause these events.

SAGITTARIUS A*

Ionized gas

Our **SUN** has completed just **20 orbits** of the **GALACTIC CENTER** in its **4.5 BILLION** year **LIFE so far.**

The Andromeda Galaxy is our largest neighbor. Wider than the Milky Way, but lower in mass, it is expected to merge with our galaxy in 10 billion years.

OUR GALACTIC BACKYARD

The Milky Way is orbited by about 50 satellite galaxies—most of them tiny, barely visible dwarfs. There are also two nebulae—the Large and Small Magellanic Clouds. This whole group circles a point halfway between us and the Andromeda Galaxy (and its satellites). With them, the smaller unbarred spiral Triangulum Galaxy makes up our Local Group.

TRIANGULUM GALAXY

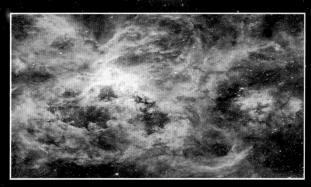

This star-forming region is in the Large Magellanic Cloud. The LMC is traveling fast enough, probably, to pass right through our galactic neighborhood.

SOLAR SYSTEMS

A massive red star goes supernova, sending a shockwave of newly created elements rippling through deep space. The disturbance starts a chain reaction that may eventually ignite another star—which could then form a planetary system.

Spun flat by a young star's gravity, a disc dense with gas and dust grains whirls furiously. In a close-up (inset) of the Orion Nebula, two stars are possibly in the early stages of forming such protoplanetary discs.

ORDER FROM CHAOS

The new protostar's gravity pulls a denser ring of gas and dust closer. It is almost ready to start fusing hydrogen. Meanwhile churning dust grains are already clumping, or accreting, together in the ring. Some gain enough mass to begin attracting smaller particles to them, becoming protoplanets. When these reach 20 Earth masses they are able to accrete gas too.

Hydrogen and helium suck onto the planets, which balloon in mass. But the race is on. When the star ignites, its solar winds will blast away any remaining gas, halting the growth of these newborn gas giant planets.

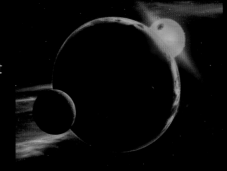

Planets in a cool red dwarf system receive a fraction of the sunlight we do. Those close enough to be warm would also be tidally locked — that is, one side is fixed facing the star and endlessly baked.

Brown dwarfs are often found with what seem to be protoplanetary discs. In 2005 a gas giant 15 times bigger than Jupiter was discovered orbiting brown dwarf 2M1207 in the constellation Centaurus.

The nearest known planetary system to Earth is Epsilon Eridani. Here at least two massive planets each shepherds an asteroid belt, much like Jupiter does in our Solar System. The strong gravity from these planets prevents the asteroids from clumping together to form another planet.

Planets like **NEPTUNE** are **thought** to form **LAST** from **gas** and **ice** at the **EDGE** of the **DISC.**

DEBRIS DISC

When all the gas is used, the minerals and ice grains left in the protoplanetary disc carry on churning and clumping to form asteroid-like planetesimals. These might collide, either smashing into fragments or gently wobbling and merging to grow bigger.

The circumstellar ring of dust around Vega is thought to be from a recent planet collision, within the last million years.

After millions of years, the loose debris is all gone. A handful of bodies remain. They are now massive enough to "spherize" and make ball-shaped terrestrial (rocky) planets like our Mercury, Venus, Earth, and Mars.

MULTIPLE SUNS

Sun-like stars in our galaxy are most commonly seen in twin, or binary, systems. Planets have been found orbiting either each single binary star or, if they are close twins, both stars—a circumbinary orbit. Even triple and quadruple star systems exist. However our theories suggest that the gravity arrangements in such multi-star systems are so complex, that any planets which tried to form would be ejected.

Kepler-47 is a binary star system known to have two orbiting planets. The brightest star, Kepler-47A, is a similar mass to our Sun and 84% as luminous. Its partner star, Kepler-47B, is a dim red dwarf only one-third the Sun's mass. Both planets are roughly Neptune-sized and probably gas giants.

ALIEN PLANETS

Kepler 10 b was the first-ever confirmed rocky exoplanet. It orbits Kepler 10, a star like ours, but 20 times nearer than Mercury is to our Sun. Kepler 10 b would be 20 times hotter than Mercury!

A way from the Solar System, the first extra-solar planet, or "exoplanet," was found in 1991. Many more alien worlds have since been discovered—some far stranger than anticipated.

PLANET FINDING

The first exoplanets were discovered as interruptions in the radio signals from dead stars called pulsars. Astronomers now have an array of tools to find and examine exoplanets.

To gauge a planet's size, a telescope measures dips in a star's brightness caused when the planet crosses (transits) in front of it. A close-orbiting planet's mass causes minute swaying movements in its star's spin speed, or radial velocity, due to gravity tugging by the planet itself. Gravitational microlensing—the way stars "bend" light around them, to magnify what lies beyond—is used to detect planets with a wide or long-distance orbit, known as a long period.

The star Kepler 10 also has an outer gaseous planet, 10 c, twice the size of Earth.

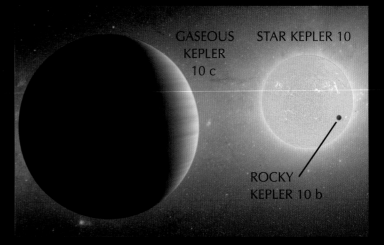

GASEOUS KEPLER 10 c

STAR KEPLER 10

ROCKY KEPLER 10 b

Giant planet HD 189733 b appears deep azure under the light of its star. Fierce, scorching winds whip up condensing droplets of silicates—"glass rain." This scatters red light and reflects blue.

The radial velocity method led to the discovery of many so-called "hot Jupiters." These are supermassive gas planets found unexpectedly close to their parent stars. They are thought to form farther out and migrate inward. Hot Jupiters have their atmospheres burnt away, eventually revealing a rocky core.

WASP-12 b is a type of "puffy" gas giant whose atmosphere has been inflated by solar and internal heating. It orbits so close to its star, it is being consumed. Three times larger than Jupiter and 40% of the mass, WASP-12 b most resembles a gigantic Saturn. It will be gone in 10 million years.

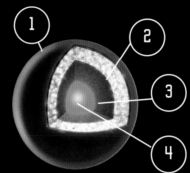

Radiation-blasted pulsar planets are thought to be made from supernova dust that gathered in a protoplanetary disc around a remnant, white-hot neutron star.

A possible "diamond planet," Neptune-sized 55 Cancri e is thought to be rocky and have a carbon-rich makeup, like its star.

55 CANCRI E

1. **GRAPHITE SURFACE** Carbon
2. **DIAMOND LAYER** Another form of the element carbon
3. **MANTLE** Silicon-based minerals
4. **PLANET CORE** Molten iron

CHEMICAL WORLDS

To determine a newly found world's composition, and possible atmosphere, astronomers use a type of asteroseismology. This analyzes ripples in light waves from the planet to measure what is inside. Also, absorption spectroscopy studies how a planet's atmosphere absorbs starlight that shines through it. Analysis of exoplanet HD 209458 b, a hot Jupiter, discovered hydrogen, oxygen, carbon, and water evaporating from its atmosphere.

Host stars are measured for the heavier elements they absorbed during their original formation, that is, their level of metallicity. Stars rich in oxygen and silicon would be expected to create terrestrial planets like ours. Much rarer super-metal-rich carbon stars might form terrestrial planets made partially of diamonds!

> **By 2014,** over **2,000 STARS** were **known** to have **EXOPLANETS** with **500** being **multi-planet SYSTEMS.**

Exoplanet GJ 1214 b is 2.7 times Earth's diameter and seven times more massive. It orbits close to a red dwarf and may have 446 °F (230 °C) clouds of potassium chloride or zinc sulfide.

Methuselah, or PSR B1620-26 b, may be one of the oldest planets in the Universe. It orbits a pulsar and white dwarf binary in the globular cluster M4, near the heart of our galaxy.

Coldest exoplanet so far discovered is OGLE-2005-BLG-390L b. Five times bigger than Earth, it orbits a cool red dwarf. If rocky, it would be a mega-chilly –370 °F (–223 °C) at the surface.

LOOKING FOR LIFE

Kepler's search area was carefully chosen to be above the obscuring dust lanes of the Milky Way, and in an area that would never be crossed by the Sun. More than 3,500 stars with planet candidates (inset) were found.

The search for exoplanets is centered on Sun-like stars, in the hope of finding another place in our galaxy where complex life might exist.

Kepler Space Telescope being made at NASA

"GOLDILOCKS" ZONE

In 2009, NASA launched an orbiting telescope dedicated to searching for Earth-sized planets that might lie in the habitable or "Goldilocks Zone" of their stars. Over four years, the Kepler planet-hunter was trained on 150,000 targets in a star-rich portion of the sky near the Cygnus constellation. Kepler viewed planets transiting stars up to 3,000 light-years away, enabling astronomers to gauge planetary size and mass.

Once gas giants had been eliminated, 1,696 potentially rocky planet candidates remained. Further observations revealed 51 were orbiting in or near the "Goldilocks Zone." The mission ended in 2013 when the spacecraft's stabilizing devices failed, hampering its ability to maneuver. However analysis of Kepler's data will continue for years.

Kepler uses an array of 42 CCDs (charged coupled devices) in its photometer, 90 times more powerful than an average camera.

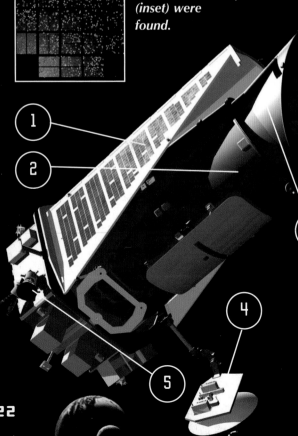

KEPLER SPACE TELESCOPE

1. **SOLAR ARRAYS** Convert sunlight to electricity
2. **PHOTOMETER** Telescope designed for narrow-field, deep-sky observing
3. **SUNSHADE** For temperature and light-swamping protection
4. **HIGH-GAIN ANTENNA** Narrow-beam, directional Earth communication
5 **TWIN STAR TRACKERS** Keep Kepler aligned toward target stars

"Soon we will know if the galaxy is full of planets like Earth, or if we are a rarity."

John Grunsfeld, associate administrator, Kepler Mission

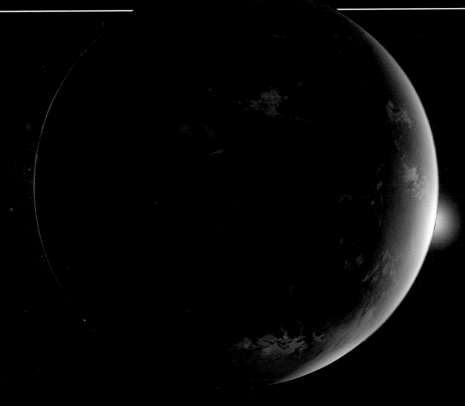

Two-fifths larger than Earth, Kepler-62 f is the most similar exoplanet to our home world yet found. Its mass and composition are unknown, but it lies in the outer part of the habitable zone of its yellow dwarf star. The zone is much smaller than in our Solar System, the star having 69% the mass and 64% the radius of our Sun. Kepler 62 e, a possible superVenus that orbits closer in, can be seen to the right like a "morning star."

If **KEPLER** could have **viewed** its **TARGET SUNS** from **more** than **one ANGLE**, it might have **DISCOVERED** **22,000** more **super-Earths**.

On the baking-hot surface of Gliese 667 Cc you would see three suns, the nearest being a red dwarf. There are estimated to be tens of billions of rocky worlds orbiting low-mass M-class red dwarfs.

LIKELY SUSPECTS

The most likely life-hosting planets are "super-Earths" up to twice our size—estimated to be the upper limit for rocky planets. However, these larger-mass worlds may not be like ours. If Earth had not evolved natural greenhouse gases to warm its climate, the temperature would be $-2\ ^{\circ}F$ ($-17\ ^{\circ}C$).

Our atmosphere came partly from outgassing volcanoes. Would higher gravity on a super-Earth compress and seal the surface, making volcanoes impossible?

We have discovered that the Milky Way is almost certainly teeming with planets. Experts are sure that, with better tools, we will soon find habitable ones.

EARTH   KEPLER-62 E   GLIESE 581 G   GLIESE 667C C   KEPLER-22 B   TAU CETI E

These five planets are super-similar to Earth. The more massive ones could well be waterworlds, where the higher gravity forces water into the planet's mantle and raises surface ocean levels to completely cover any land.

FUTURE MISSIONS

It is over 40 years since humans last ventured beyond Earth orbit. NASA aims to land astronauts on an asteroid by 2025 and send a human mission to Mars sometime in the 2030s.

When fully developed, NASA's upcoming Space Launch System will be able to carry 10% more payload than Apollo's Saturn V.

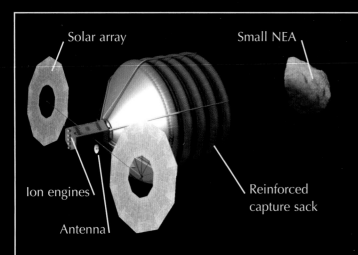

Solar array

Small NEA

Ion engines

Reinforced capture sack

Antenna

To ensnare a Near Earth Asteroid, NASA plans to send a remotely operated space tug equipped with a 50-foot (15-meter) diameter capture bag. The electric ion-engined craft would take four years to reach the NEA.

ASTEROID CAPTURED

Having secured and stabilized a tiny 23-foot (7-meter) Near Earth Asteroid, NASA would redirect the pilotless space tug (capture craft) to orbit our Moon. A crewed mission would then intercept the orbiting craft and NEA. The crew's mission would take at least 20 days. It is planned as a technological feat and stepping-stone for future Mars trips.

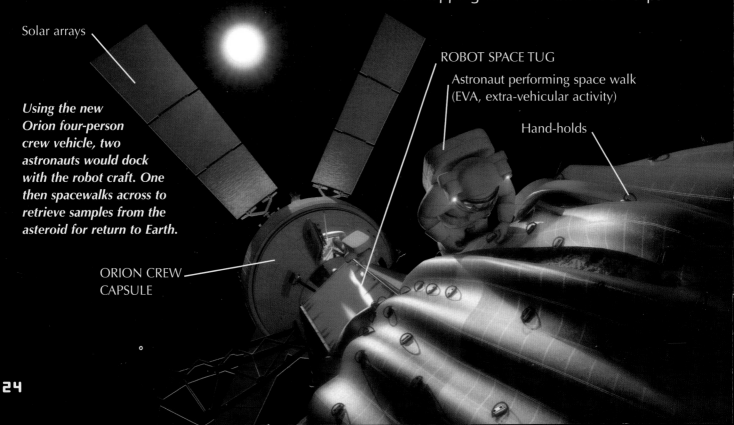

Solar arrays

ROBOT SPACE TUG

Astronaut performing space walk (EVA, extra-vehicular activity)

Hand-holds

Using the new Orion four-person crew vehicle, two astronauts would dock with the robot craft. One then spacewalks across to retrieve samples from the asteroid for return to Earth.

ORION CREW CAPSULE

ORION DEEP SPACE CREW VEHICLE

1. **NASA ORION COMMAND CAPSULE**
2. **SERVICE MODULE** Provided by European Space Agency
3. **FUEL STORE**
4. **MAIN ENGINE**
Single rocket to power craft out of low Earth orbit

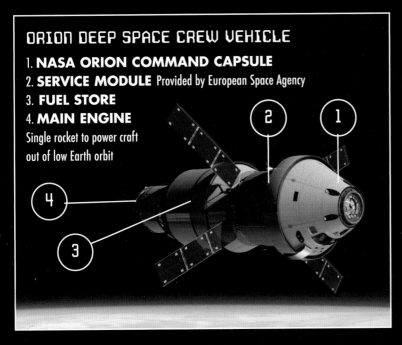

An artist's concept of a NASA Mars lander is based on commercial SpaceX's Dragon capsule. Doubling as a habitat, the crew landing vehicle would be 40 times more massive than anything landed before.

HUMAN PLANETARY MISSIONS

The first extraterrestrial planet that humans visit will be Mars. But missions to the Red Planet face daunting obstacles. Mars' orbit is elliptical (oval), meaning one launch window every 26 months. The journey would take nine months with current propulsion technology. This exposes the crew to dangerous cosmic radiation and the physical effects of prolonged zero gravity. The spacecraft would need to carry a large amount of fuel, including for landing. The mission team has a minimum of three months on Mars before a launch window back to Earth is available.

Radiation, isolation, propulsion, and contamination are challenges humans must meet before we set foot on an alien world.

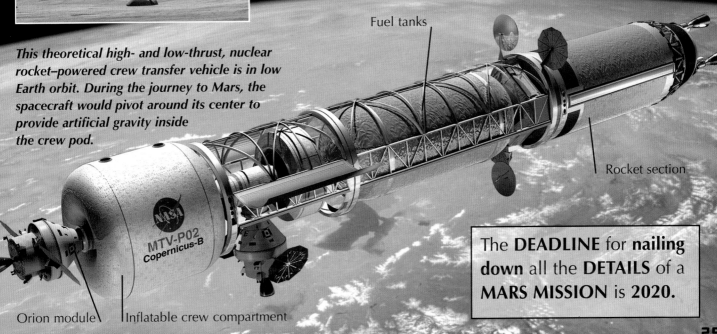

This theoretical high- and low-thrust, nuclear rocket–powered crew transfer vehicle is in low Earth orbit. During the journey to Mars, the spacecraft would pivot around its center to provide artificial gravity inside the crew pod.

Fuel tanks

Rocket section

MTV-P02
Copernicus-B

Orion module

Inflatable crew compartment

The **DEADLINE** for **nailing down** all the **DETAILS** of a **MARS MISSION** is 2020.

COLONIZERS

Lunar soil is full of oxygen and minerals. Colonizing the Moon would be a great first step in moving our human species off-world.

BUILDING A MOONBASE

The Moon would make an ideal base to launch human missions into the Solar System. Observatories might be built on the rocky far side of the Moon, which is also rich in the element helium 3—fuel for possible fusion reactors. Lunar soil's 42% oxygen could be extracted to breathe, and it also has useful amounts of silicon and iron.

Scientists using 3D-printing technology have successfully built

Transporting building materials to the Moon would be very expensive. This NASA concept shows an advanced party of robotic rovers 3D-printing basic dwellings with concrete made from lunar soil.

large structures with simulated lunar dirt. But "printed" colonies should be sited at the Moon's poles, where the day-night temperature differences are less extreme. Also at the poles is abundant water-ice trapped in deep craters.

NASA has developed a whole series of roving vehicles that could operate on either the Moon or Mars.

3D-PRINTED MOONBASE

1. **INFLATABLE DOME**
Pressurized, encloses habitation module
2. **OUTER DOME** Weight-bearing, protective, hollow closed-cell structure
3. **SKYLIGHT** Micrometeoroid shield
4. **ENTRANCE/AIRLOCK**

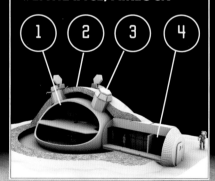

This European Space Agency concept shows a multi-dome base being completed by robot rovers 3D-forming rock domes over the last of the uncovered pressurized modules.

A MARS COLONY

The Red Planet would be a hard place to visit, let alone live on. Mars One, a private venture, intends to send four astronauts to start a colony by 2025. The difficulties of fuel and logistics means the trip is a one-way ticket, funded from reality TV rights.

There has been no shortage of applicants. They need to be tough. Mars has a carbon-dioxide rich atmosphere 97% thinner than Earth's, and an average temperature of −131 °F (−90 °C). Dust storms can last for months, preventing the use of solar power.

This future NASA Mars outpost would be a forerunner and test-bed before any permanent settlement by any space agency.

Martian dust may even be toxic to humans.

The plan is for intelligent rovers to scout a flat site that has water-ice. Cargo landers then arrive, with rovers to prepare the colony. The estimated setup costs vary from $6 to $20 billion.

MARS ONE SETTLEMENT

1. **LIVING UNIT** Inflatable modules, living quarters, and storage
2. **LANDERS** Used as bathrooms
3. **HALLWAYS** Connect lander units after being installed by colonists
4. **GREENHOUSE** Unshielded portion of a living unit for growing food
5. **SOLAR PANELS**

On **MARS**, colonists would be **vulnerable** to **charged particle PROTON STORMS** from **deep space** which, unlike **SOLAR STORMS**, cannot be **predicted.**

Fifty years from now? Mars One colonists melt ice in the soil to extract drinking water and to make oxygen. Soil piled on living units absorbs solar and cosmic radiation, but this danger strictly limits time outside. Four more crew land every two years to grow the colony.

Rover ① ② ③ Airlock ④ ⑤ Equipment shelter

PIONEERING CREW LANDER

GOING INTERSTELLAR

At 4.24 light-years away, Proxima Centauri is our Sun's nearest starry neighbor. A spacecraft equipped with today's most advanced nuclear rocket would get there in about 85 years.

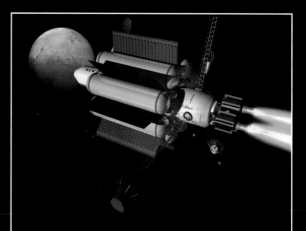

Atomic-powered hot plasma engines are the most advanced propulsion technology in the near future. VASIMR engines could cut the journey time to Mars from over two years to five months. But even that would be hopelessly slow for interstellar travel.

PROBLEMS OF SCALE

The idea of gathering data on another solar system from nearby has always been exciting. In the 1970s a team in the United Kingdom set about designing a probe that could reach a star within a scientist's lifetime—50 years.

Project *Daedalus* used a theoretical fusion rocket to zap, each second, 250 deuterium/helium-3 fuel pellets with high powered lasers, crushing them into fusion. The energy from this "mini-star" was contained and directed out the back by a powerful magnetic field.

The ship itself, with its massive load of fuel and huge engines, would be assembled in orbit. The first stage would then burn for two years before sending the second stage to one-eighth the speed of light for a 47-year coast to Barnard's Star. Unable to brake, *Daedalus* would launch probes as it flashed past the star. Data and images would arrive at Earth 27 years later.

DAEDALUS PROBE

1. **SHIELD** Beryllium with projected cloud of charged particles
2. **PROBE BAY** Telescopes, sensors, and remote probes. Also houses robotic repair "wardens"
3. **PROPELLANT TANKS** Deuterium and helium-3 pellets
4. **LIQUID HYDROGEN STORE** Used as coolant
5. **REACTION CHAMBER** Made of molybdenum TZM—a metal alloy that retains strength below −238 °F (−150 °C)
6. **COILS** Superconducting coils to contain plasma energy

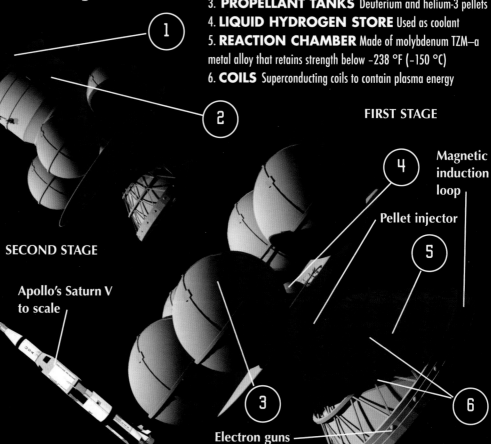

FIRST STAGE

SECOND STAGE

Apollo's Saturn V to scale

Magnetic induction loop

Pellet injector

Electron guns

> *"Faster than light? We know from studying the early Universe, nature can do it. The question is, can we do it?"* NASA physicist Harold G. White

It is 2070. An antimatter-drive ship carrying a crew has arrived at star Alpha Centauri B, 4.37 light-years from Earth. The ship accelerated to 98% of light speed, making a journey time of just five years. The crew was towed miles behind the gamma-ray-emitting engine and protected by a shield. Droplets of coolant were sprayed ahead of the engine to vaporize oncoming debris. Mid-coast, the ship was flipped around and the engine fired to deccelerate. A vast umbrella of Mylar layers deflected oncoming debris.

PLANET ALPHA
Centauri B b

VALKYRIE ANTIMATTER SHIP

1. **MYLAR UMBRELLA** Ready to open
2. **SECOND COIL** For return journey
3. **CREW SECTION** With shuttle lander
4. **TETHER** Approximately 10 miles (16 km) long
5. **SHADOW SHIELD** Made of thick tungsten
6. **PROPELLANT TANK** Matter and antimatter flakes derived from hydrogen kept at near absolute zero
7. **ENGINE COIL** Ejects plasma from atomic accelerator

> For every **YEAR** traveling near the **SPEED OF LIGHT, three years** would **pass** on **EARTH.**

Alcubierre's theoretical Warp Drive uses the tendency of spacetime to bend toward massive objects. It creates a "warp bubble" caused by negative mass generated from exotic matter—hypothetical substances that do not fit natural laws.

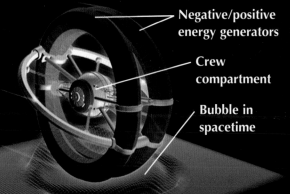

Negative/positive energy generators

Crew compartment

Bubble in spacetime

THEORETICALS

Combine matter and antimatter and their mass is turned into energy. Today's science can produce only tiny reactions. Enough antimatter to propel a ship like *Valkyrie* would need the energy output of entire humankind for the next 40 years.

According to Einstein's theories, traveling faster than light is impossible—except perhaps during the Big Bang, when particles may have broken this barrier. Following this theory, generating enough negative mass could contract spacetime, the very fabric of the Universe, in front of you, and expand it behind you. In effect, you would travel faster than light while remaining still. Such a warp drive breakthrough could take us to nearby star systems in months, perhaps even days.

A ship enters the negative mass of a wormhole—a possible tunnel between two different points in spacetime.

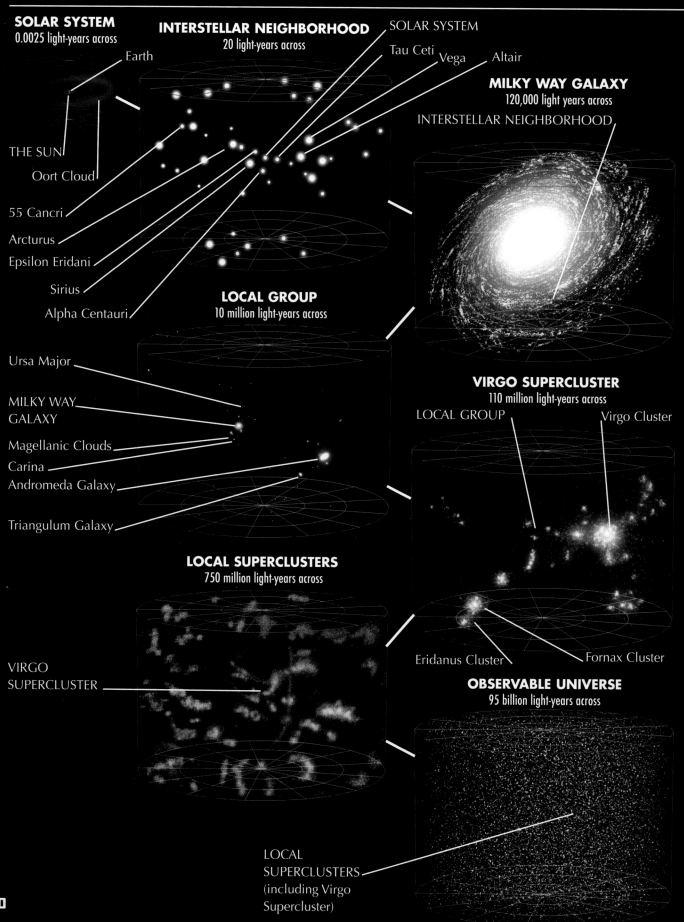

SOLAR SYSTEM
0.0025 light-years across

Earth

THE SUN

Oort Cloud

55 Cancri

Arcturus

Epsilon Eridani

Sirius

Alpha Centauri

INTERSTELLAR NEIGHBORHOOD
20 light-years across

SOLAR SYSTEM

Tau Ceti Vega Altair

MILKY WAY GALAXY
120,000 light years across

INTERSTELLAR NEIGHBORHOOD

LOCAL GROUP
10 million light-years across

Ursa Major

MILKY WAY
GALAXY

Magellanic Clouds

Carina

Andromeda Galaxy

Triangulum Galaxy

VIRGO SUPERCLUSTER
110 million light-years across

LOCAL GROUP Virgo Cluster

LOCAL SUPERCLUSTERS
750 million light-years across

VIRGO
SUPERCLUSTER

Eridanus Cluster Fornax Cluster

OBSERVABLE UNIVERSE
95 billion light-years across

LOCAL
SUPERCLUSTERS
(including Virgo
Supercluster)

GLOSSARY

ASTEROID relatively small, rocky, or metallic space object orbiting the Sun; most are between 33 feet (10 m) and 620 miles (1,000 km) across

ATMOSPHERE layer of gases around a space object such as a planet

BINARY STARS two stars relatively close together, orbiting each other around a point between them that is the center of mass of both of them

COMET relatively small space object following a long, lopsided orbit around the Sun that warms and glows when near the Sun

DWARF PLANET space object that orbits a star but has not cleared its orbit of other large objects

ELLIPTICAL oval-shaped, as in the orbits of many planets, or the shape of many galaxies

FUSION in nuclear fusion, parts of atoms combine or join and give off energy, as when hydrogen atoms fuse into helium in the Sun

GRAVITY force of attraction between objects, which is especially huge for massive objects like planets and stars

MANTLE middle region, between the crust and core, of a planet, moon, or similar space object

MASS amount of matter in an object, in the form of numbers and kinds of atoms

MOON space object that orbits a planet. The single moon of Earth is usually known as the Moon (capital letter M)

ORBIT regular path of one object around a larger one, determined by the speed, mass, and gravity of the objects

PLANET large space object that has a spherical shape due to its gravity, and has cleared a regular orbital path around a star

SATELLITE space object that goes around or orbits another, including natural satellites like the Moon orbiting Earth or Earth orbiting the Sun, and man-made satellites

STAR space object that at some stage is large and dense enough, with enough gravity, to undergo fusion and give out light, heat, and similar energy

INDEX